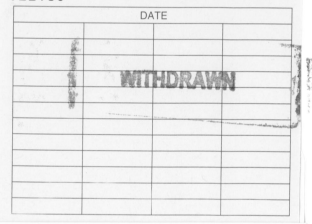

Earth-Friendly Crafts With Nuts and Veggies in 5 Easy Steps

Anna Llimós

Enslow Elementary

an imprint of

Enslow Publishers, Inc.

40 Industrial Road
Box 398
Berkeley Heights, NJ 07922
USA

http://www.enslow.com

Note to Kids and Parents: Getting earth-friendly materials is easy to do. Just look around your house for containers, wrappers, and other things you would throw out. Some of these recyclable materials may include plastic, paper, cardboard, cork, and cloth. The materials used in this book are suggestions. If you do not have an item, use something similar. Use any color material and paint that you wish. Use your imagination!

Safety Note: For some of these crafts, you will need special tools. Ask an adult to help you complete these crafts.

Enslow Elementary, an imprint of Enslow Publishers, Inc.

Enslow Elementary® is a registered trademark of Enslow Publishers, Inc.

WARNING: The crafts in this book contain materials to which people may be allergic, such as nuts.

Translated from the Spanish edition by Stacey Juana Pontoriero.
Edited and produced by Enslow Publishers, Inc.

Library of Congress Cataloging-in-Publication Data
Llimós Plomer, Anna.
  [Vegetales (2006). English]
  Earth-friendly crafts with nuts and veggies in 5 easy steps / Anna Llimós.
      p. cm. — (Earth-friendly crafts in 5 easy steps)
  Translation of: Vegetales / Anna Llimós. — 1a ed. — Barcelona : Parramón Paidotribo, 2006.
  Includes bibliographical references and index.
  Summary: "Provides step-by-step instructions on how to create fourteen simple crafts using nuts, dried vegetables and leaves, beans, and other plant materials"—Provided by publisher.
  ISBN 978-0-7660-4191-2
  1. Nature craft—Juvenile literature. I. Title.
  TT157.L52513 2013
  745.5—dc23
                            2012013434

Future edition:
Paperback ISBN 978-1-4644-0313-2

Originally published in Spanish under the title Vegetales.
Copyright © 2006 Parramón Paidotribo-World Rights
Published by Parramón Paidotribo, S.L., Badalona, Spain

Production: Sagrafic, S.L.
Text: Anna Llimós
Illustrator: Nos & Soto

Printed in Spain
112012 Indice, S.L., Barcelona, Spain
10 9 8 7 6 5 4 3 2 1

To Our Readers: We have done our best to make sure all Internet addresses in this book were active and appropriate when we went to press. However, the author and the publishers have no control over and assume no liability for the material available on those Internet sites or on other Web sites they may link to. Any comments or suggestions can be sent by e-mail to comments@enslow.com or to the address on the back cover.

Contents

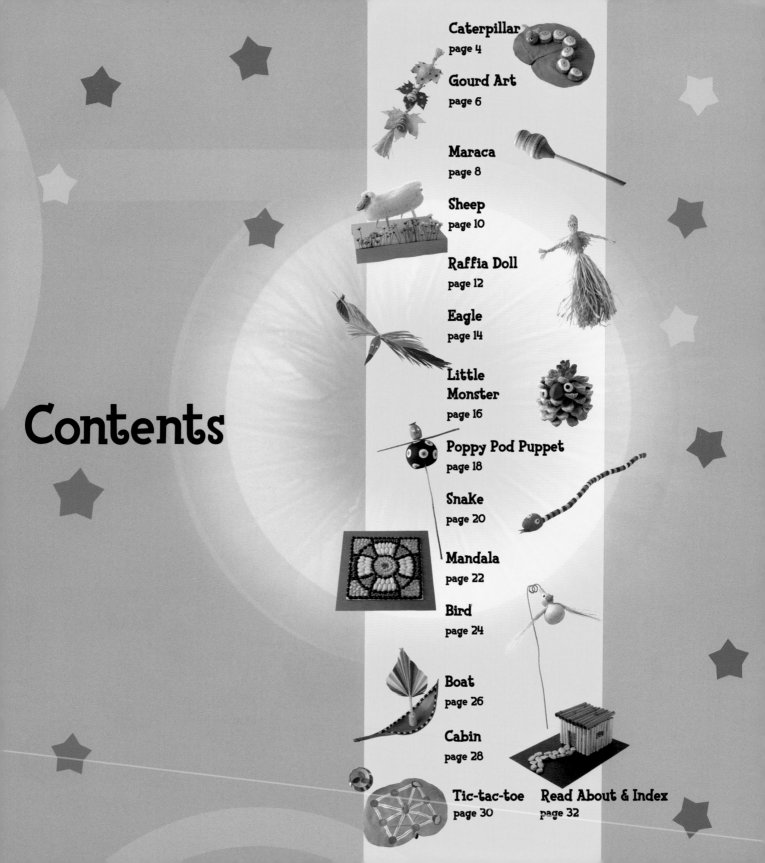

Caterpillar

MATERIALS

dry leaf
paint-different colors
paintbrush
4 walnuts
raffia
scissors
white glue

1 Paint the dry leaf. Let dry.

2 Open three walnuts and remove the insides. Paint the six nutshell halves. Let dry.

3 Decorate the nutshells as you wish. These nutshells will form the caterpillar's body.

4 For the head, paint eyes, a nose, and a mouth on a whole walnut. Glue some raffia onto the head to make hair. Let dry.

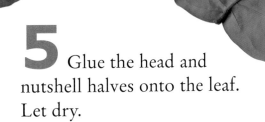

5 Glue the head and nutshell halves onto the leaf. Let dry.

A nutty caterpillar!

Gourd Art

MATERIALS

3 dry leaves
paint-different colors
paintbrush
3 small craft gourds
raffia
scissors
white glue

1 Paint the dry leaves any way you wish. Let dry.

2 Paint the craft gourds any way you like. Let dry.

3 Tie a long bunch of raffia together.

6

4 Tie a strand of raffia to each leaf.

5 Tie the gourds and leaves along the raffia bundle. You may also add glue to keep everything securely in place.

Just hang it up!

7

Maraca

MATERIALS

1 craft gourd, split in half
beans
white glue
paint-different colors
paintbrush
air-drying clay
1 bamboo stick

1 Put some beans inside one of the gourd halves.

2 Glue the other gourd half on top, sealing the beans inside. Let dry.

3 Paint the gourd as you wish and let dry.

4 Stick a piece of clay on one end of the bamboo stick. Shape it into a cone.

5 Glue the gourd to the flat side of the clay. Let dry.

Shake it!

Sheep

1 For the sheep's legs, stick the four toothpicks into the loofah. You can add a piece of toothpick for the tail, if you wish.

2 For the sheep's head, draw a face on the peanut with black permanent marker.

3 Cut a piece from the loofah to make the ears. Glue it to the head and let dry.

4 Glue the head to the body. Let dry.

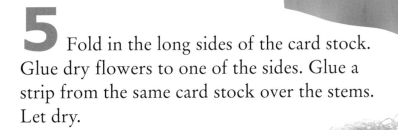

5 Fold in the long sides of the card stock. Glue dry flowers to one of the sides. Glue a strip from the same card stock over the stems. Let dry.

Baaa, baaa!

Raffia Doll

1 Tie a bunch of raffia together in the middle. Take a smaller, shorter bunch of raffia of another color. Tie it to the bigger bunch. Braid the shorter bunch for the hair.

MATERIALS

raffia–different colors
scissors
2 black-eyed peas
1 corn kernel
3 lentils
white glue

2 Tie a strand of raffia below the braids to create the head. For the arms, braid a few pieces of raffia on each side below the head.

3 Wrap a different color of raffia around the bunch to make the body.

4 Wrap the braids around the head and tie them back.

5 Glue two black-eyed peas onto the head for the eyes. Glue the corn kernel to make a nose. Glue three lentils onto the body for buttons. Let dry.

A special doll

Eagle

MATERIALS

1 dry pointy leaf
paint
paintbrush
2 dry palm leaves
raffia
scissors
white glue

1 Paint the pointy end of the leaf. Let dry. This is the eagle's beak.

2 Paint the eyes. Let dry.

3 For the wings, paint the tips of the palm leaves. Let dry.

4 Tie the wings together with a piece of raffia.

5 Glue a piece of raffia underneath the head. Glue the head to the wings. Let dry.

What spectacular wings!

Little Monster

1 pinecone
paint
paintbrush
1 large hazelnut
2 small hazelnuts
white glue

1 Paint the pinecone and let dry.

2 Add details if you like.

3 For the nose, paint the large hazelnut. Let dry.

16

4 For the eyes, paint the two small hazelnuts. Let dry.

5 Glue the eyes and the nose to the pinecone. Let dry.

What will you name your little monster?

Poppy Pod Puppet

MATERIALS

1 craft gourd
craft drill (Ask an adult!)
paint-different colors
paintbrush
1 dry poppy pod
1 thin stick
raffia
white glue

1 **Ask an adult** to drill a hole into the gourd. Paint it and let dry.

2 Decorate the gourd any way you wish.

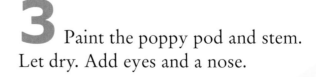

3 Paint the poppy pod and stem. Let dry. Add eyes and a nose.

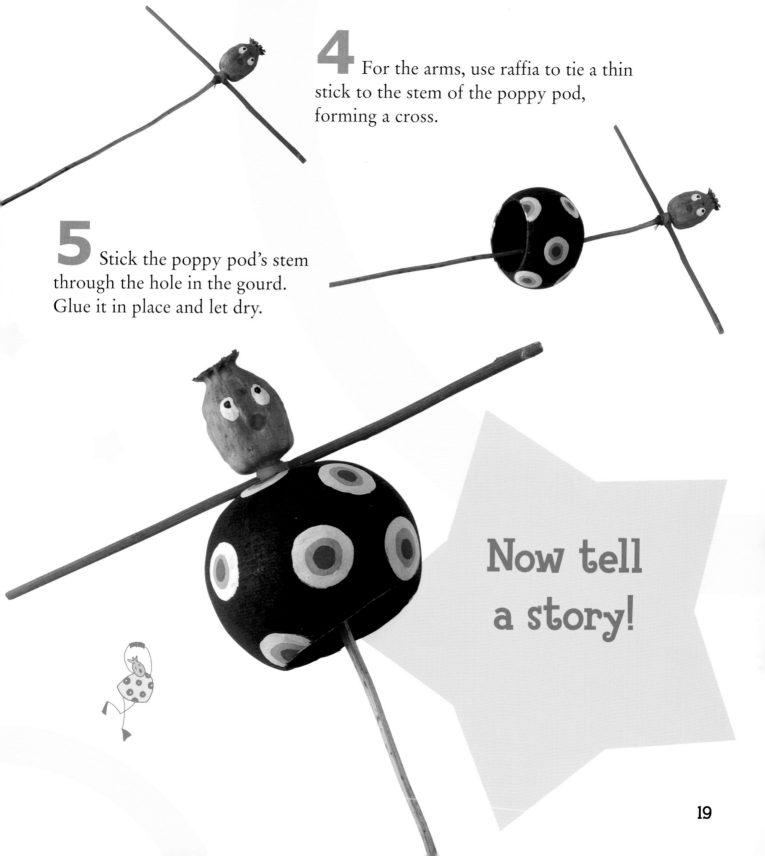

4 For the arms, use raffia to tie a thin stick to the stem of the poppy pod, forming a cross.

5 Stick the poppy pod's stem through the hole in the gourd. Glue it in place and let dry.

Now tell a story!

Snake

MATERIALS

1 thin twig
paint
paintbrush
1 almond
red card stock
scissors
white glue

1 Paint stripes on the twig and let dry.

2 Add different colored stripes if you wish.

3 For the head, paint the almond and let dry.

4 Paint the eyes on the almond. Let dry.

5 Cut out a tongue from the red card stock. Glue it underneath the head. Cut one end of the twig at an angle. Glue the head to the angled end of the twig. Let dry.

What a cool looking snake!

Mandala

MATERIALS

card stock—white and another color
scissors
compass
pencil
black beans, corn kernels,
mung beans, lima beans,
lentils, or other beans
white glue

1 Cut the white card stock into a square. Use a compass to draw a circular design on it.

2 Glue the black beans along the lines. Let dry.

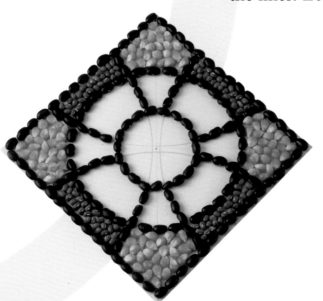

3 Glue corn kernels into the spaces in the corners. Glue mung beans into the spaces in between the corn kernels. Let dry.

4 Glue lima beans and lentils into the spaces next to the corn kernels and mung beans. Let dry.

5 Glue corn kernels and mung beans inside the center circle. Let dry. Glue your mandala onto a sheet of colored card stock. Let dry.

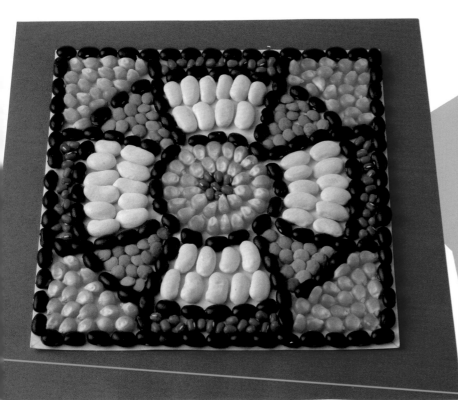

Try different designs!

Bird

MATERIALS

1 small craft gourd with the stem
black permanent marker
air-drying clay
white glue
2 ears of wheat
scissors

1 Draw eyes on the upper part of the gourd with black permanent marker.

2 Model a beak from clay.

3 Glue the clay beak to the gourd. Let dry.

4 Cut off the stems from two ears of wheat.

5 Glue an ear of wheat to each side of the gourd to make the wings. Let dry.

What a cute little bird!

Boat

MATERIALS

1 cork
paint-different colors
paintbrush
scissors
1 dry palm leaf
1 dry large leaf
black beans
dry corn Kernels
white glue

1 Paint the cork and let dry. Poke a hole into it with the scissors.

2 Paint the dry palm leaf and let dry. This is the sail.

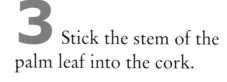

3 Stick the stem of the palm leaf into the cork.

4 Glue beans and corn kernels along the edges of the large dry leaf. Let dry.

5 Glue the cork with the sail onto the large leaf. Let dry.

Sail away!

Cabin

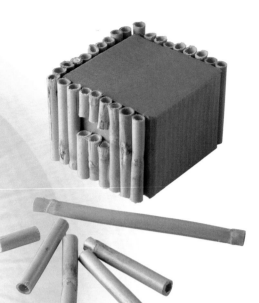

MATERIALS

bamboo sticks–different sizes
square cardboard box
white glue
mung beans
watercolors
paintbrush
black card stock
fava beans

1 Glue the bamboo sticks to the walls of the cardboard box, leaving spaces for the door and window. Let dry.

2 Glue mung beans into the spaces for the door and window. Let dry.

3 Paint as many bamboo sticks as you need for the roof. Let dry.

4 Glue the bamboo sticks to the roof. Let dry.

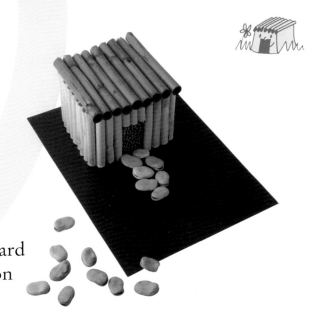

5 Glue the cabin onto card stock. Glue the fava beans on the card stock to make a walkway. Let dry.

What a great cabin!

Tic-tac-toe

1 Paint a tic-tac-toe box on the leaf. You may draw the one with the nine boxes or use this one with the lines. Let dry.

MATERIALS

1 large dry leaf
paint—different colors
paintbrush
6 pumpkin seeds
1 craft gourd

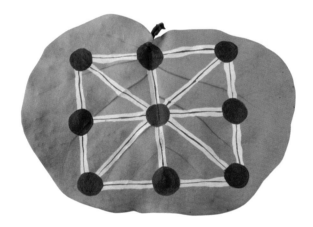

2 If you are using the box with the lines, paint circles on the nine points where the lines meet. Let dry.

3 Decorate the circles as you wish.

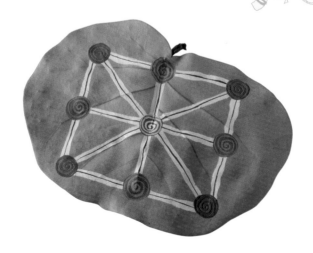

4 For the game pieces, paint three pumpkin seeds one color and the other three pumpkin seeds a different color. Let dry.

5 Paint the gourd as you wish. Let dry. Keep the game pieces inside.

Who wants to play?

Read About

Books

The Bumper Book of Crafty Activities: 100+ Creative Ideas for Kids. Petaluma, Calif.: Search Press, 2012.

Evans, Katie. *Cool Crafts for Hip Kids.* New York: Price Stern Sloan, 2012.

Hardy, Emma. *Green Crafts for Children.* New York: Ryland Peters & Small, 2008.

Internet Addresses

Busy Bee Kids Cafts
<http://www.busybeekidscrafts.com/>

FamilyFun: Crafts
<http://familyfun.go.com/crafts/>

Index
Easy to Hard

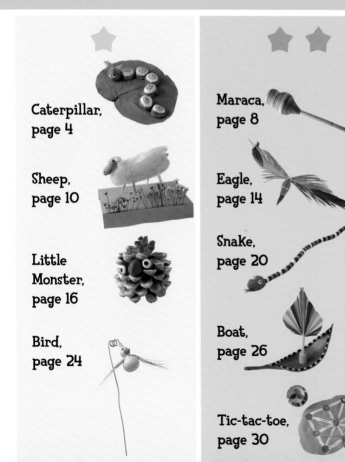